A Few More Masonic Sermons

By

Thomas E. Poole and Bascom B. Clarke

Copyright © 2020 Lamp of Trismegistus. All rights reserved. No part of this publication may be reproduced or transmitted in any form or by any means, electronic or mechanical, including photocopying, recording, or by any information storage and retrieval system, without permission in writing from Lamp of Trismegistus. Reviewers may quote brief passages.

ISBN: 978-1-63118-436-9

*Foundations of Freemasonry
Series*

Other Books in this Series and Related Titles

A Few Masonic Sermons
by A. C. Ward & Bascom B. Clarke (978-1-63118-435-2)

Royal Arch, Capitular and Cryptic Masonry
by various authors (978-1-63118-425-3)

Masonic Symbolism of Easter and the Christ in Masonry
by various authors (978-1-63118-434-5)

Masonic Symbolism of King Solomon's Temple
by Albert G. Mackey, David Harlow & Robert Smailes
(978-1-63118-442-0)

Psalms of Solomon by King Solomon (978-1-63118-439-0)

The Two Great Pillars of Boaz and Jachin
by Albert G. Mackey, H. L. Haywood, William Harvey & others
(978-1-63118-433-8)

Masonic Symbolism of the Apron & the Altar
by various authors (978-1-63118-428-4)

Lost Chapters of the Book of Daniel and Related Writings
by Daniel (978-1-63118-417-8)

Cloud Upon the Sanctuary by K. Eckartshausen (978-1-63118-438-3)

Symbolism and Discourses on the Entered Apprentice, Fellowcraft and Master Mason Blue Lodge Degrees by various (978-1-63118-413-0)

The Lost Keys of Freemasonry or The Secret of Hiram Abiff
by Manly P. Hall (978-1-63118-427-7)

The Story and Legend of Hiram Abiff by William Harvey, Manly P. Hall & Albert G. Mackey (978-1-63118-411-6)

Audio Versions are also Available on Audible and iTunes

Table of Contents

Introduction...7

The Creation of Light
by Thomas E. Poole...9

Note...27

A Sermon on Being a Man
by Bascom B. Clarke...29

A Sermon on Honesty
by Bascom B. Clarke...35

A Sermon on the Heart of a Man
by Bascom B. Clarke...39

A Sermon on Guarding the Doors
by Bascom B. Clarke...45

A Sermon Given at the Scottish Rite
by Bascom B. Clarke...49

Introduction

From the beginning of Modern Freemasonry's birthdate of 1717, the intelligentsia of humanity have found refuge for safe reflection within the walls of the fraternity. Masonic writers have produced a nearly incalculable amount of written musings on a multitude of esoteric and philosophical subjects, as they relate to the ancient mysteries that Freemasonry currently storehouses. Sadly, most of it appears to have sat largely unread, as American Freemasonry in particular, continues to transform itself into something that bears little resemblance to what it was originally designed to be. The true essence of Freemasonry is not that of blind patriotism or a single-minded national religion but one of Universal Brotherhood and altruism, designed for the betterment not just of its members but of society as a whole. In particular, for those who are not members of the fraternity, as Freemasonry has always acted as a beacon, to help guide humanity through darker times, with the hopes that one day we will collectively reach a truly enlightened age.

It's not uncommon for new members joining the fraternity to find little education within the walls of many modern lodges, in spite of so much written material available to the membership. Many older members are not simply uneducated with regards to real Masonic history and symbology, not to mention the vast arena of related subjects, but they are disinterested in all of it, as well.

Lamp of Trismegistus is doing its part to help preserve humanity's Masonic history by making some of these classics available to those students who are seeking to unearth the knowledge of these ancient colossi. As such, Lamp of Trismegistus offers its readers highlights of Masonic study, culled from a variety of authors and viewpoints, with the hope bringing education back into the fraternity. So, be sure to check out other titles in our *Foundations of Freemasonry Series* as well as our *Esoteric Classics*, *Theosophical Classics*, *Occult Fiction* and our *Christian Apocrypha Series*, and don't be afraid to let a little altruism into your own heart or even into your Lodge. You can also download the audio versions of most of these titles from iTunes or Audible, for learning on the go.

The Creation of Light

By Thomas Eyre Poole

"And God said, Let there be Light, and there was Light."

No Christian, and particularly no Christian Mason, who seriously reflects upon these words, can think of them without the liveliest emotions of profound veneration!

Whether the Momentous Occasion, on which they were uttered; the Divine Being, who gave the sublime command; or the Blessed Object, which they called forth, be considered, Created Intelligence must admire adoringly, and praise its Almighty Author, with godly fear.

In the unexampled scene before us, the power and goodness, the wisdom, mercy and love of Omnipotency, are, in a striking manner, magnificently displayed, and Deity shines forth in all the grandeur of His Might.

We are instructed in the 2nd verse of this chapter, that "the earth was without form and void "and darkness was upon the face of the deep;" but that "in a moment, in the twinkling of an eye," the voice of God was heard throughout the universe, Let there be Light!" and the first great principle of life and energy possessed and pervaded the unformed mass! Moreover, that from that instant the mighty work of this world's creation, with all its varied productions and inhabitants, advanced in beauteous order and progressive perfection! And, though last in formation, yet first of all below in superiority, Man came forth, to use the sweet, expressive language of the pious BISHOP HEBER, "fresh and unclad from his Creator's Hand."

Now without wishing, in the least, to draw any unnecessary comparison between ourselves and other Christians, I cannot but observe, and press the observation upon our most attentive consideration, as Masons, the eventful transaction recorded in our text; because it presents to us more, perhaps, than the generality of mankind, a most impressive lesson of Instruction. And that lesson, if duly attended to, will convey to us a comprehensive and practical groundwork for the constant and profitable exercise of our minds and hearts in the pursuits of both speculative, or scientific, and operative, or religious Masonry.

Before, however, deducing such reflections as our present meditations may draw from an examination of the subject before us, it will be well to take, as a necessary and introductory step, a short view of the Three characteristic features which it supplies, and which will disclose most interesting, and profitable subjects of holy instruction to the pious and intelligent brother.

And 1st: - the Occasion, on which these words of the One Almighty, Creative Spirit, the "I am," that "was, and is, and is to come," were spoken.

It was the Creation of this vast and sublunary globe which we inhabit, together with everything that "lives and moves and hath its being." The Mighty Architect of all things had already prepared, as we read in the 1st verse of this chapter, the elements of a natural world. Nevertheless, they slept, as yet, without motion, silent and in disorder, until the Divine World gave the Fiat; and, lo, sudden light burst in mid-day splendor upon them! It was then, that there instantly succeeded Action, Sound and Harmon; and animated all things!

How apposite and impressive is the religious moral, which is hereby taught us! Look at the state of things, before Light was made! Fit and striking emblem of man's spiritual darkness, before illumined and quickened by the Spirit of Grace! Oh, what a high value ought we to set on that more ineffably glorious and eternal light, which comes from the Bright and Morning Star of Redemption, through His precious Gospel of Salvation; and which only can dispel that darkness from our souls, in which sin and corruption have mantled them! As in the material, so is it in the soul, that world of never-dying thought and reflection; how void! how dark! how motionless, whilst deprived of spiritual light!

Possessing, as did all the properties of matter every quality to fit them for the several purposes, for which their Beneficent Creator formed them, yet we see their powers and faculties lay dormant and inert, unable to move into active existence, or answer their respective ends, before Light was produced.

Now, what a subject of serious reflection does Creation, again, supply to the thoughtful Brother, in this, its primeval state of being, the very womb of its infancy! For, if we think, as we ought to think, with pious wonder and due thankfulness on this act of mercy and power, which thus lit this world, buried in unproductive darkness, into what it now is, teeming with all the diversified treasures of God's bounty — the blessed effects of material light; how much more should we admire; and, what is of far greater consequence, with what diligence and earnestness should we seek after that new creation of spiritual light in the soul by the Sanctifying Author of regenerating and quickening grace, which alone can remove, and keep removed, the darkness of sin which naturally benights it. Surely we ought to pray to the Eternal source of Divine Light to incline and assist us in storing up in our hearts and minds the monitory instructions here afforded us; that we may not be forgetful by what agency our sinful hearts are renewed, our darkened minds illumined, our whole man transformed, and all the fruits of the creation of Grace implanted in our souls! For, consider, I beseech you, what must, and will be, that darkness in us, which is the sad, but inevitable consequence of Original Transgression, if that sweeter, yet not less powerful voice of Saving Mercy sounds not within us (oh, that it may continually sound in us with the same happy effect,) "Awake, thou that sleepest, and arise from the dead, and Christ shall give thee Light!"

And whose is that voice, which does so often speak to us in after-time, not, as in the Beginning, with the awful sublimity and fear-inspiring majesty of Deity, creating; but gently, and affectionately, and mercifully moving our sluggish dispositions, stirring up our unwilling inclinations to receive Life and Salvation into our souls? It is the same, that was in the beginning; for, "in the Beginning was the Word, and the Word was with God, and the Word was God, Yes, it is God, but God Incarnate, The Light of the World!"

The conviction of this Truth brings us, in order, to that next striking feature of our Text; the Divine Being, who gave the high command in the words before us. That no one but God, could have given it, is evident to all of us, who believe in the Bible; and that the Everlasting did positively utter it, is no less certain. With what consoling hope then, and exalted confidence, ought we to adore that mighty author of all things in His Power, which could thus call them into existence; in His Goodness who not only made, but fitted them in their first estate for so much happiness; in his Wisdom, who so excellently framed and disposed them for their several and distinct ends; and in His Mercy and Love, who, having created, blessed and pronounced them to be the objects of His peculiar and providential care.

To us, my Masonic Brethren, who are so frequently reminded of these glorious attributes of Omnipotence, and on whose attention they are so constantly impressed, the Omnipotent Source of both Temporal and Spiritual Light, should be an object of our dearest and highest regard. A godly fear, a grateful heart, a chastened veneration, and a mind embued with a hallowed love for such a Being, ought ever to shed their improvinging influence throughout the whole of our lives and conversations.

And, if in the responsible nature of created Intelligences, how much more so in that of redeemed Creatures of Immortality should we be diligent to let these fruits of revealed light bear their unequivocal testimony in our hearts and consciences, that we are not in Name and Word only, but in Spirit and in Truth, the Sons of Light. For these are evidences of sincerity and consistency, which cannot be gain-sayed; the only true tests by which, as Masons, we should most rigorously prove ourselves, whose whole system in all its machinery, speculative, or operative, inculcates the Belief in, and Worship of One, True and Omnipotent God, in His Threefold characters of Father, Son and Holy Ghost: insists upon our entire trust in Him; and most solemnly directs us to prove our Faith and Sincerity by the improvement of our hearts and minds to His Glory and the good of mankind.

Having considered the Divine Being, who spoke the remarkable words of our Text, we may go on to the consideration of the Third characteristic feature of it, namely the object, Light.

This inestimable and blessed gift of the Creator claims our particular attention, as Christian Masons, in whatever point of view we notice it.

It would be an inquiry, too foreign to the design of a discourse like this, to enter into a copious explanation of the

Philosophy of the Science of Light; yet, it may not be, altogether, without some practical benefits, thus to take a passing glance at it.

Light, in its most extensive signification and use, may refer to various objects; and be differently defined. Scripturally viewing it in relation to Things and Time, it may be classed under Three Heads; Material Light, as in the Creation of the world; Moral Light, as in the Mosaic Economy; and Spiritual Light, as under the Gospel Dispensation from the Birth of its Heavenly Author to the end of Time.

When it is spoken of definitely and in relation to Persons, we perceive, it is used with less freedom and more caution. Indeed, it then immediately assumes the prerogative of sacredness in the highest degree. For, we read how John the Baptist is, by way of eminent distinction, called a burning and a shining Light, as the fore-runner and Messenger of the Messiah. But, by no Being, not even the highest and first of the spirits in Heaven; by the Triune God ALONE in His indivisible and never-to-be confounded nature of Father, Son and Holy Ghost, can this noble appellation be employed in that definite and solemn sense, in which we find it in the Sacred Volume. "I am the Light" is an affirmation, too Omnipotent and Hallowed, to be pronounced except by Deity Himself.

The properties of Light, and their fitness for producing not only beneficial effects in the natural, or material world, but likewise the powers they possess for the display of God's Omnipotency and glorious attributes, are further subjects deserving our reflection and examination, as tending to raise in Masons a becoming and constant sense of the value and necessity of this quality, in those things which are spiritual and have relation to the future and immaterial world. It may not be out of place, therefore, to recommend to your private meditations those remarkable events, set down in God's Word, of this display and effect of Light by The Light, as in the miraculous shining of it on the face of Moses after his descent from Mount Sinai: the translation of Elijah in the midst of it alive to heaven; the Transfiguration of our Blessed Lord, in company with these two in the clouds: and the over-powering manifestation of it in the conversion of the persecuting Saul! Such facts, considered in connection with the subject matter of the text, cannot, with the Lord's blessing, be unattended with the most favorable results to personal edification.

To these considerations another one may be here added, before we leave this part of the subject. It is the striking circumstance, not, perhaps, generally noticed, yet very useful in its practical application, namely, the precedence of time given to the creation of material Light. We know that, not until the fourth day, were the Lights set in the firmament of the heavens, or the Sun and Moon made to rule the day and the night. How easily may we extract from this single fact, a fund of rich spiritual and moral instruction! And that instruction I am satisfied, cannot be more significantly conveyed to us, than in the spirit and sentiment of the truly excellent Bishop HALL, who dwells largely and practically on this very point: I am not aware, that he was one of the Fraternity; but the pious comparisons of holy instruction he institutes on this subject, must be always very serviceable to the best interests of the Craft.

In his First Contemplation on the Work of Creation, in general, he remarks on the striking gradation of it. God, he says, could "have made "all the world perfect in an instant," but would not. And, not only does He take time in forming it, but does it also by degrees: neither makes anything at first, or, at once, absolute; but first things without life, then those which should have life and being, and lastly those which have being, life, and reason; and so with ourselves; first the life of vegetation, then of sense, and reason afterwards. With such an example "how vainly" he adds, do we hope to be perfect at once. It is well for us, if through many degrees we can rise to our consummation." And, then, the Bishop passes on, in a similar strain, to the Creation of Light, of which he says; "Whence, O God, was that first Light." - "Thou madest the Sun, madest the Light without the Sun, before the Sun, that so Light might depend upon Thee, not upon thy creature." - "How plainly wouldst Thou teach us "that one day we shall light again without the Sun; thy presence shall be our Light, Light is sown for the Righteous, - "that light which Thou shalt once give us shall make us shine like the Sun in glory." "O be Thou our Sun unto which our Light may be gathered!"

From all that has been advanced, and from what we are taught, and instructed in by the Lectures and Workings of our Lodges, we see, that Masonry, in the most sacred sense, is a Science of Light; a bright beam, a noble and holy System of practical Religion, which derives its excellence from, and would ever direct its children to the First Grand Source of All Light, The Mighty God, the Everlasting Father, the Prince of Peace! How, then, do we endeavor to, and how ought we to regard and be affected by it? Did we embrace, and do we estimate it, professedly and abstractedly, without concern about its internal, excellencies, which, if duly practiced and studied according to our time, and abilities, must help us to, be the better Christians? Did we unite ourselves with it, or do we behave, as if we united ourselves with it, as a mere society to be desired and followed solely for its exclusive charity and peculiar Mysteries? Heaven forbid! At our Initiation we professed to believe; and we have been, in the course of our regular advancement, subsequently taught and made to know, that the Principles of our Order are founded upon the never-failing base of Revealed Light or True Religion. And we cannot moreover, forget, how imperatively it insists upon and prizes the daily practice of every Social, Moral and Religious virtue. It is, consequently, our most serious duty, as Professors of this Light, to, undeviatingly comply with its important, excellent and solemn obligations.

The more, indeed, we consider and enter into the true spirit of the Craft, which has, let me repeat it, for its aim, the Glory of God and good of one another, the more will our minds be illumined and our hearts improved by the holy wisdom and virtue, which it delights to cherish and diffuse throughout its Members. Nor is it over-coloring the moral beauties of the Order neither raising, it on too elevated a pedestal of superiority, to say of it, in relation to those, who enroll themselves in it, that Christianity and Infidelity are not more incapable of union, than a Good Mason and a Bad Man. The combination of such contradictory characters is as impossible, as the Agreement of Light with Darkness!

By no class, or denomination of Christians, therefore, more than by Ourselves, should the Force of those Practical Reflections, deducible from a review of the Text, be felt and converted to Self-Improvement in righteousness and true holiness; and, for many reasons. Two only of these, I shall now mention: and First, from the very circumstance of that Secrecy, which conceals from ordinary notice our various proceedings.

This Principle of Our Order, advantageous as it is, and indispensably essential to all the Interests of our Society, has exposed, as Civil and Ecclesiastical History will shew, and may expose the Fraternity of Free and Accepted Masons to much suspicion, however unmerited; and even, as several of us have personally witnessed, to ignorant contempt. For censorious curiosity will ever be most captious and ready to take offence, when it is most disappointed. And this, I trust, will satisfy us, that we have the strongest inducements held out to us from this prominent and peculiar rule of our Society, to guard ourselves and Institution from the shafts of invidious malice on the one hand; and from the more poisonous and fatal darts of detracting ridicule on the other, by exhibiting in our general conduct that spirit and behavior, which will show, that, be the principles and rules of the Science of Light, what they may, by which, as Masons, we are governed among ourselves; THIS, at least, is manifest, that we are not of the number Of THOSE, into whose souls hath not shined the Saving Light of the Gospel of Truth.

Necessary and Lawful as Secrecy and Mystery are, under due restrictions; sanctioned as they are by the Divine Author of all Light in the religion of our most holy faith; embracing, as they do in the laudable objects of Masonry, the promotion of virtue and increase of human happiness; unobjectionable as they are thus proved to be, when not infringing upon, but resting on the Broad Altar of Christian principles and devoted Loyalty; yet, the exhortation I am now giving you, is both necessary and seasonable. For, as in Christianity itself, so in Masonry, by the most natural and easy analogy, objections and oppositions will often assail a system, admirable as it may be in its design, perfect in its arrangements, and faultless in its doctrines, which cannot be known except by a due and solemn course of preparation. Hence, the wisdom and duty of Masons to be watchful, that their Light, or Good, be not evil-spoken of.

But not alone from the fact of Mystery, which veils our operations, throwing around our Forms and Ceremonies an Allegorical, and, to the Uninitiated, an unintelligible, but to us a Moral and Spiritual meaning, are we as Masons, necessitated to govern ourselves by the pure and spiritual light of the Gospel. Without this heavenly influence, Masonry, and indeed, everything however sacred and excellent, would be as sounding brass and a tinkling cymbal. Yet, although I adduce this, as one, and a most weighty reason, for the greatest circumspection in our religious deportment, lest we bring shame and discredit on our Ancient Institution, I would now stir up your consciences to a stricter course of Morality and Piety, for the time to come, by the consideration of our Masonic Obligations.

These, we all well know, the Seal of Fidelity, never to be broken but by death, stamps under the inviolable fold of Silence; but they remind us, as Masons, that we should account most dear, and practice most diligently, those precepts, which arise out of a subject, so sublime as that of the Creation of Light, considered in all its bearings, and which it teaches and enjoins.

How can we, who profess to value, above all things, that Light, "which shineth more and, more unto the perfect day;" who, in a manner, which we are forbidden to disclose, study and engage to rule, ourselves by it, neglect, or altogether set at nought those ways of holiness and paths of instruction which this Light so plainly defines and sets before us? Faulty, - I will speak it in stronger terms, - sinful will be that inconsistency, which we shall thus exhibit to the world; sharp and merited will be, sooner or later, the stings of that bitter reproach, which will overtake us, who, knowing these precepts have such an intimate affinity with our Masonic obligations, presume to slight, much more, heedlessly to violate them!

Such are a few of the general Practical Reflections, which the subject matter of the Text suggest. Many more, equally applicable and instructive, might be introduced. But I sincerely hope and pray, that these will be sufficient to make us see and feel, consider, how we will, the three great lessons of Holy

Wisdom hereby taught, that they bear most forcibly upon our faith and practice. Still, on an occasion like the present, so rare and interesting, which brings us together not only, I trust, for charitable purposes, but also for the delightful duty of unitedly worshipping, to our edification, the All-wise Architect and Geometrician of the universe, to be contented with merely praising or defending a society, whose intrinsic excellence will speak for itself to us, who know its usefulness would be to lose sight of the chief end of our appearance here. For the same cause, we should do wrong to satisfy ourselves with too broad deductions of morality, inapplicable to, perhaps, or scarcely touching, upon, ourselves as individuals: for, we should neglect the most efficacious method of self-improvement.

In bringing, therefore, our meditations to a close let us look narrowly into our own hearts, each one, for himself, and judge ourselves by a more pointed rule of self-examination, in respect to our Masonic Duties, how far we have, or have not, according to the Light imparted to us, squared our actions with one another on the level of those principles we profess, and kept our desires and passions within the proper compass of Masonic rule and Christian practice.

Alas, my Brethren! In the retrospect of the past year, I fear the review of it will not be entirely without a mixture of regret. Much cause as we, undoubtedly have, for humble gratitude to God for the prosperity of the Craft in the increase of its numbers, in the kind, generous, and condescending patronage of the representative of Sovereignty: and in the advancement of its general interests, yet candor compels us to confess that, in not a few instances, we have lost sight of some of the most vital principles of our Order, which we are therein taught.

It is, I know, and feel, a delicate, nay, a painful and ungrateful task; yet is it a bounden duty, so to particularize our own errors and sins, as to bring them more directly home must "judge ourselves, if we would not be judged."

Now one, and the First Masonic Duty I will call it, in the observance of which sadly remiss, is that of Morality. And, yet, on this obligation, as we well know, Masonry lays an unusual stress. Not only does she herein recommend the moderate and sanctified use of all the gifts and blessings of Light: but, in the very spirit of the Gospel, that Revealed Light from heaven, directs us to "keep our bodies in subjection to the Will of God;" to restrain our passions; and to "mortify the flesh with the affections and lusts:" taking her authority from Scripture for the same: which tells us "we are not our own but bought with a price."

Let any of our brethren, therefore, who may, unhappily, have been guilty of willful and continued acts of intemperance and excess, reflect seriously how they are not simply breaking their Masonic vows, but also their Christian obligations of Love and Obedience to the Will of God; and henceforth begin to walk more worthy of the Sons of Light.

But there is another and important duty, the very common and condemnatory transgression of which bespeaks an inexcusable indifference to one of the most binding, and noble precepts of our Order. I mean, the respect for and protection of each other's characters, and those of our families, when unjustly and unprovokedly assailed. These, we are conscious, the noble principles of Masonry requires us to hold most dear, and, as sacred as our own. Around the reputation of Her Children, Masonry casts a consecrated Robe, which she forbids her followers to touch, much less tear off with unnecessary rudeness. And, when compelled by Honor and Justice to do so, she bids us with a tear of Pity, not a smile of malice, to be merciful. And is not this echoing back the very voice of the Gospel, which teaches us to "speak evil of no man." So the immortal Poet and greatest Moralist this world beheld, instructs mankind. And, no one, who is not dead to the nobleness of the human character, or insensible to the finest feelings of his nature, can hear of, or see, without just anger and praiseworthy indignation, a Christian command and Masonic Obligation of unspeakable consequence, so wantonly violated, as is often witnessed. For the sake, therefore, of all that is lovely and of good report, let us, as much as lieth in us, have a conscience void of offence towards Man and God.

Were these Two leading Obligations of Our Order more faithfully and diligently observed, we should not behold many of our Fraternity losing sight, so sadly, as they do, of the VIRTUES OF LIBERAL SENTIMENT and RELIGIOUS TOLERATION, so nobly and so wisely encouraged by our August Sovereign Herself. I speak, perhaps, too boldly for a few, but I trust a few only, at all events I know, I speak, as I ought to do. These unfailing signs and tests of an expanded mind and Christian heart, the finest traits in every, but especially the Masonic character, have ever and deservedly commanded the respect and esteem of the reflective portion of mankind; and they are among the first principles of the Science of Light. Bear and Forbear in all the relative situations and circumstances of Life, but particularly in matters of RELIGIOUS differences, are axioms of Wisdom, which the best and wisest of men have loved to promulgate and practice. Ought, then, any of us, who are Masons, to reject, or even slight, so Heavenly a Principle? No. Rather, let us be more solicitous and ready to act, for the future, on that comprehensive, yet well-guarded freedom of admission to our Order of all religious denominations of Christians, the door of which is closed against none, save those of absolute Infidelity and bigoted Scepticism!

There is another subject for individual improvement, which I would briefly advert to; and it is the respect, with which ourselves and families should ALWAYS SPEAK of MASONRY. No matter, indeed, what the Society or Institution be which we join, provided it be good, in its peculiarities. As to the rule of conduct I am going to recommend, it will usefully apply to all alike; and it is this: - When once we have associated ourselves with it; when once we have voluntarily and unsolicitedly, deliberately and solemnly enlisted under its banners, and engaged to uphold it in WORD and DEED; it is the duty (and they who disregard it, are faithless to their pledge,) neither to speak evil of it ourselves, nor suffer others to do so with impunity, if we can prevent it, in a Christian manner. Above all things, not to use our best efforts to suppress such unmasonic behavior amongst those, who are more immediately under our domestic government, is to manifest, on our parts, an unworthy indifference, as Brethren of the Order. Not to the Mason himself alone, but to every member of his family the habit of depreciating the Craft, should be always an unknown offence. If any of a Mason's circle cannot think well of it, if for no worthier motive than that of prudence and decorum, they will do well to "set a seal upon their lips" that they "offend not with their tongue."

Thus shall we, as Christian Masons, adorn the Fraternity by our behavior; and afford to the world a practical evidence of the soundness of those principles, which direct and govern us. Thus shall we, prove by the most conclusive arguments, those of upright conduct and pious conversation, that God, who spoke in the Beginning and commanded the Light to shine out of darkness, hath not spoken to us in vain by His Son, Jesus Christ, the Light of the Moral and Spiritual world. And, furthermore, by thus strictly observing the Rules of Right and Wrong, we shall illustrate more fully than by the amplest explanation, what is of most consequence to be understood and prized by every one of us.

NOTE

In the following sermons by Bascom B. Clarke, the writer employs a writing tactic, in which his sermons are all written in the form of a discussion or a lesson, to a fictional student of his, named Ezra. So, when you see that name come up, you may mentally replace it with your own name, or any other name you choose, if you like.

A Sermon on Being a Man

By Bascom B. Clarke

There's another thing that Freemasonry teaches that's mighty good doctrine, Ezra. The true Mason's word is just as good or a little better than his bond. Masonry teaches its votaries to be good, upright, just and true, not only in the letter but in the spirit of the understanding in dealing with all mankind.

It doesn't matter much who you are or where you are going, Masonically speaking, just so you re a man, Ezra. You've got to be "Eleven feet high and walk in the middle of the road," son, that's all.

Masonry doesn't give a rip whether you're a Hindu or a Hottentot, where you come from or who your daddy was, just so you can stand the Bertillion measurements of manhood, all the way from the crown of your head to the soles of your feet. When Solomon, King of Israel, entered into a compact with Hiram, King of Tyre, and with the "Widow's Son" it was one of the few gentlemen's agreements written across the pages of history that has stood the storms and the sunshine of centuries, that has outlived its enemies, that has swept the world for humanity and for God.

There may be — there are those who don't love us, who say all manner of evil against us, who accuse us of crimes and of being law-breakers, of being horse thieves and scoundrels, and why? For the same reason what a Methodist looks with contempt upon the devoted Catholic, that kneels in worship before her images. We of the Methodist faith were not taught that in bending the knee before the image of the "Blessed Virgin" it was but proof of faith in the Son of Mary, and of love for the Mother of Jesus. On the other hand, the Catholic, with his ritualistic dogma, smiles with pitying scorn when the Methodist stands up and with tears streaming down his cheeks confesses to having failed to follow the teachings of the same Christ which both Catholic and Methodist acknowledge as their Savior. It's the same reason that causes a Jew to sneer at Jesus being the Christ, or a Mohammedan from having faith in any God but Allah and of any prophet excepting Mohamet. Ah, the narrowness of our human souls, Ezra, the prejudice of our religions!

I once hired the best quartet in the world to sing for me at the State Fairs, where I was engaged in proselyting the business world to my faith. I also employed the best speaker and all-around clown in America, who entertained acres of people from Maine to California. The leader of the quartet and his brother were Catholic, while "Old Mack" was a shouting Methodist. In Springfield, the home of Abraham Lincoln, where the quartet lived, we passed the Catholic church where they worshipped, going to and from the fairgrounds every day. These boys never passed the church upon which the cross was displayed without lifting their hats or crossing themselves, as proof of their devotion to their church. "Old Mack" tapped me on the shoulder one day and called my attention to their devotion. That same day when preaching his "Fare-you-well

Brother Watkins" sermon before five thousand people, old "Mack" let the reefs of his main-sail slip and forgot where he was. With that multitude standing spell-bound before this grand old man, who was preaching the real salvation for sinners, these boys in the quartet almost laughed him to scorn. When he had finished, he wept for joy, but the leader called him a "damned fool." That is the kind of toleration that causes men, through ignorance, to call us names, Ezra.

I used to hear the Masonic brethren called horse thieves by some who didn't like than, and who said all manner of evil against them. One of these old boys, in his fatherly interest in me, told me of the many crimes which the Masonic fraternity had committed against God and humanity, which had gone unpunished. And when I asked him why, he told me they were too strong in number, that whoever tried to bring them to justice would die by their hands! Ah, ignorance and superstition and falsehood! Thou hast stalked abroad and misled men in the years a gone! Ah, infamous slanderers, to what depths have you descended to malign an order which has been and ever will be the foundation of all religions! To one who has drunk of the Masonic cup of knowledge almost to the last drop, who wondered if these falsehoods could be true of men who gladly go at midnight to relieve the sufferings of others, without thought of fee or reward, and who has found among them men belonging to all religions, devoutly kneeling at the altar of Freemasonry asking God's blessing on friend and foe alike, what slander!

I've been preaching the gospel of Freemasonry, realizing that to a certain extent in doing so I am violating one of the most sacred tenets of the order, silence. "Set a watch, oh Jehovah before my mouth, and keep thou the door of my lips!" Forbid that I should undertake to defend this order, whose grand characteristics need no defense, which has stood the storm of centuries and brought within its gates the greatest and the best men this world has ever known, from John the Holy Baptist, forerunner of the Nazarene, to the disciple whom Jesus loved and who rested upon His breast at the Last Supper, if indeed not the Savior himself!

It's human to resent imputations against us which are not true, and in my old-fashioned Methodist way, I let the governor belt fly off once in a while, Ezra, but I just can't help it. When I hear a man telling a falsehood, knowingly or unwittingly, about a friend of mine, I want to tell him of it, and shake my fist under his nose while doing so. I once had a very dear friend, who was a Knight of Columbus, and another very dear friend who was a Knight Templar. I heard another Knight of Columbus accuse this Knight of Columbus friend of mine of having taken advantage of, and of having wronged a Brother Knight Templar. That was a mixed-up religious mess, wasn't it, Ezra? Well, I knew that it was a mistake, and then and there I defended my Knight of Columbus friend from an attack from his brother in the faith, concerning my brother in the faith!

It takes a man in the middle of the road and eleven feet high to stand up and be counted sometimes, Ezra, but the grace of God, the love and fellowship of the Holy Spirit will descend on you like a benediction from on high, if you'll follow this injunction: "As ye would that others do unto you, do ye even so unto them."

A Sermon on Honesty

By Bascom B. Clarke

Masonry never contemplated having to deal with "crooked limbs" in the wood choppin', Ezra. Masonry was organized strictly according to the code of a "gentleman's game." When you buy a stack Masonic beans and light your cigar, and the other fellows do likewise, or mayhap their cob-pipes with death rattles in the stems, loaded with Adams' Standard, you are not supposed to strain your eyes trying to read your neighbor's hand. Neither is he supposed to have to shut his hand up dead tight with just enough of the corners exposed to enable him to "read 'em and weep."

I never liked the idea of being like a settin' hen, ready to peck at everybody who wondered how many eggs she might have in her nest. Masonry is a close corporation, and a close communion church, when it comes to meddlin' with the working tools, but the first and last leaf in Masonic jurisprudence teaches us to "act on the square." Do you follow me, Ezra?

Whenever you find a man who goes through life on a general denial, it pays to examine him adversely before the trial. That's according to the sublime principles of Blackstone. Moreover, whenever you find a man proclaiming his honesty from the house-tops, he's just rocking the cradle to sell his own conscience. Why should I offer advance proofs of my good intentions when nobody has accused me of anything, Ezra? It's like taking a band of Indians from Carlisle University to advertise Sagwa.

That reminds me of a story. Many, many moons ago, there came to the little village where I once lived in Old Indiana, one of these "Sagwa" dispensers or "roots, herbs and barks" brought from the famous Ban Yan tree of South America, I think it was. Anyhow, he located this medicinal tree as far away from home as he could. Maybe it was in Patagonia, where every prospect pleases and only man is vile enough to eat missionaries whom we sent thither to spread the gospel to the heathen in "furin parts."

The old boy who managed the hippodrome from Tomah was a trifle "pot-gutted" and wore a sombrero with hair cut on the bias, and they called him "Doc." Did you ever stop to think how many folks are called Doc, Ezra? They are like the Captains and Colonels, down south, or the professors up north. Well, this Old Doc had some likely looking bucks with his show, who spoke mighty good English when not on guard. "Rattlesnake Dick" was the bad man from Cheyenne, who, Doc told the audience, could split a postal-card at twenty paces with his three dollar Quackenbush. It just so happened that I also owned another "Quack" of the same pattern, only mine didn't have any globe sights on and Rattlesnake's did. When Old Doc challenged the world to an equal of his deadshot, he took in a little too much territory. I never sold Sagwa, or posed as a Bison William or Johnnie Baker in the use of weapons, Ezra, but I used to snuff a candle without much effort or run up a string of bull's eyes and generally got my turkey at all the shootin' matches. So a friend of mine got Doc to challenge me to shoot with Dick. I shot. We waived the formalities of splitting postal-cards, and proceeded to plug bull's eyes. After much solemn warning and more solicitude for my consenting to be the goat, we were told to "fire when ready, Gridley. Rattlesnake led off with a center-shot, and I followed suit. Then he led a trump and I made an even break. The crowd was growing hilarious at the sixth round, with honors even, when Rattlesnake fluked, missing the center an inch. I plugged number seven. Then the postal-card splitter went far a-field. Just to show respect for the audience, I plugged in ten centers without a miss and allowed it looked like rain, Ezra. It broke up the meetin'. Rattlesnake took a straight shoot across lots to the reservation, and Sagwa received a slump in Colfax.

The point I wanted to make is, that while as "Johnnie Poole" told the teacher, it pays to advertise, it's a mistake to take in too much territory in your brief of claims for recognition. Don't try to split postal-cards until you have learned to spilt stove-wood enough for your wife to get dinner with. In stating your case to the jury, Ezra, always keep this fact in mind, that the highway of truth is the only one where the traffic is never blocked, and that's the highway over which all good Masons travel.

A Sermon on the Heart of a Man

By Bascom B. Clarke

The man who seeks entrance into the order in the hope of its giving him a boost, excepting the boost of real brotherhood, — the man who seeks to commercialize Masonry, has no business even in the ante-room, where decent men are prepared for receiving the "hidden mysteries."

Did you ever read St. Paul's letters to the Ephesians and the Galatians, and the Hebrews and the rest of em, Ezra? St. Paul was a proselyte to the Christian faith. He started out to persecute them and to put them to death. Paul was a sort of Bashi-Bazouk who followed along and threw stumbling blocks in the way of the followers of the Nazarene, until one day he ran against the stone wall and was stricken blind for the time being. Then he got converted, and then he became the wheel-horse of the Christian religion. They say that a proselyte becomes the rabidest kind of a convert.

After St. Paul had gotten religion, he preached and he prayed, and when they put him in jail he wrote these letters that I'm telling you about to the faithful. In one of his latest dictations Paul wrote: "But God hath chosen the foolish things of this world to confound the wise." I never had this gospel impressed on me more than when I received an invitation one day to talk to a convention of schoolteachers. Not having ever been a schoolteacher, not even a student in a graded school during my sixty-odd years of lingering on this old sheet-iron world, I naturally wondered what this crowd of educated people had in mind when they invited me to drop over and while away an hour with them. I thought maybe they had gotten their names and dates mixed, but they assured me that such was not the case, so I concluded to look 'em over, Ezra, seeing that the first person to ever hug me after I was turned loose as an orphan to root for myself, and to push my hair back and call me nice names, was a teacher, with whom I played several return engagements ere I had grown to manhood and she to ripe old age, so I heeded the call. Did you ever start out wondering what you'd say and then find it hard to stop saying what seemed to just pour out like soap-suds running down a sink-hole? That was my name and address on this occasion that I'm telling you about. There were oodles of handsome, yes, some beautiful faces and characters present when I rang the bell for books, and just started in teaching teachers. I can't even approximate what I said, Ezra, neither could they. The boss teacher sent over to get my "Manuscript" to publish. Manuscript! Did you get that, Ezra? Well, I couldn't comply with that request, as I don't shoot paper-wads, not at teachers, if I know myself.

If you could have seen those teachers! Dignified highbrows, handsome women and pretty girls, trying to look sober and couldn't. They tittered and giggled until I had to rap for order, and me just tellin' 'em the very things which they knew better than I did. I looked back in memory to the days when I went to a country school, and told them about red-headed, stooped-shouldered Bill Parish, who drew his words out like he was afraid they'd get to fighting if he didn't keep them apart. And about Donald Brooks sitting on his buckwheat cakes to keep them warm until noon. You know, Ezra, and they knew, that a cold buckwheat cake is like eating a saddle-blanket, it's hard to masticate and harder to digest, and here they nearly threw fits laughing at their own everyday experiences as teachers. It was using the foolish things of this world to confound the wise, and I was hittin' her up on all six and gettin' encored to the echo, when I looked at the clock and found that I'd blatted a whole hour. They gave me a send-off when I closed that showed that I'd struck their funny bones, and they invited me to play a return engagement, those splendid people, the very elect of earth, who must look wise and frown on funny things most of the time, because I had dared tell them of human nature and how to handle it. It's so in Masonry, Ezra. It's the grandest and most helpful element in the world, but you must know how to gauge the doses, son. There are men who have climbed all the way up to the topmost round of the Masonic ladder and can string it out like coiling up a tape-worm on a clothes line, but they have failed in many places to observe the beautiful precepts which the Grand Architect of the Universe put into the heart of man to incorporate in the ritual.

There's an Old Boy who sweeps the streets of Madison and divides his sweepings with the sparrows who find it hard picking since the automobiles don't use oats for fuel. This old boy takes off his hat when you speak to him, and returns your salutation as a dignified gentleman should. He is polite in every way. When you drive by he gets out of the way and smiles instead of frowns. When the lodge meets, he lays aside his street clothes, dons a nifty looking suit, puts on his white apron, "the emblem of innocence and the badge of a Mason" and sits with his brethren, a gentleman and a brother clear through. You couldn't hire this old boy to blackball a candidate through spite or for a fancied grievance towards the brother who presented the petition, because in his heart of hearts, from entering the door for the first time, until his friends scatter flowers over his grave, he has been vaccinated with the spirit of Freemasonry, and it has "took, good and plenty," and his vocation in life is just as honorable as the man who wears the Master's hat, or the Templar's helmet. He's a man for a' that and a' that, and God will reward him in the Great Temple above where he may, for all we know, become one of the pilasters or the columns that help support the superstructure. It doesn't make much difference where you are along life's pathway, just so you are a man all the time, Ezra.

Masonry regards no man for his outward worth of wearing apparel, it's the heart that beats in unison with all that's good and true, with all that stands for the uplifting of mankind, and the mind that generates pure and holy thoughts, that reaches down and helps others to climb, that counts where the "Three Great Lights" burn the brightest at midnight's lowly hour, Ezra. You couldn't hope to gather together the hundred of thousands of the craft without finding a Jubelo or a Jubela or a Jubelum in that mighty army of the faithful, but you just measure 'em up with any other set of men on this great, big, cold, clammy world, and you'll find their Bertillion system equal to the best, because God has put it into the heart of man when he is chosen to a high place to try and honor, rather than disgrace his standing among men. As I have said before and am about to say again, there's an occasional ring-streaked buck among the herds, but as few or fewer according to numbers than any other institution in the world. Don't forget this gospel, Ezra. Watch and pray that ye enter not into temptation yourself, and thereby set a good example before your fellowman, for which your Heavenly Father will reward you when you have put out the fire and called the dog in life's journey.

A Sermon on Guarding the Doors

By Bascom B. Clarke

You'll find skunks in the cabbage now and then, Ezra, no matter how close you nail the pickets, or how many traps you set. Human skunks creep into Masonry, once in a while, son, just as their kinfolks creep through the hedge fence, and when you dispute their right, use their spraying apparatus to let you know how much stink they can create.

There are those connected with Masonry, I am sorry to say, who know as much about the pure and unadulterated high ideals for which Masonry stands, as Balaam's ass knew about Hebrew grammar. They get through the bars themselves by a scratch, and then for the most flimsy and un-Masonic excuses in the world, exercise the right of the black cube for pure and unadulterated cussedness, for the most flimsy excuses in the world, and, what is worse still, smile and pretend to be as innocent as unborn babes!

I'm decidedly in favor of guarding the doors of Masonry well; the very fact, that these kinds of ashlars are used for the building is the best proof in the world that the doors should be guarded. But Masonry is the great institution whose aim is to help good men to be better men, not a place where we may sneak up behind another and knife him when he can't defend himself, because we have some fancied grievance, or, what is worse still, because we don t like the man very well who has presented his petition, or because of a desire to smirch the record of those who have been entrusted with the affairs of the lodge for the time being. Of all the men for whom I have supreme contempt, it's the Mason who will go so far as to try to prevent others from advancing in the line, or from accomplishing that which I may have accomplished when entrusted with the same sacred duty, and which they have helped me accomplish. They are the Jubelums of Freemasonry. I've felt at times that these men whom we must recognize as brothers, even when they have sunk their poisoned barbs deep into our hearts, for fancied grievances, or for pure and unadulterated cussedness, were mighty poor Masonic relations, Ezra. They remind me of the fellow who couldn't lick his opponent, but who could make mouths at his sister. They are the kind who, when drunk, lick their wives just to show their authority.

I've been tempted sorely, to smite some of this class in return, while ambling down the old dirt road, Ezra, when mayhap those near and dear to me had been deprived temporarily of the "hidden mysteries," but, when I just asked God to make me very humble, and to help me to do with them as I would have them do, with me, when some of their flesh and blood were undergoing the scrutiny before being admitted, I could forget the temptation, and, looking far beyond the petty selfishness and jealousies, hear the response from "Hiram's" station, "Fair in the South," with a peace of mind that left no bitterness of soul, or self-conviction of having done a dirty trick in the dark, to avenge another trick of like nature.

I've never exercised the "right of spite," and the Mason who does is a Mason only in name, without one of the instincts of real Masonry. It ain't laying any bricks in the wall, nor furnishing any of the mortar of real old-fashioned Masonry, the foundation of all religions by preventing a good man from participating in the noble and glorious work of rebuilding the Temple of Jehovah, just because arc don't like the man who presented his petition.

They have tolerable strict rules in the regular army, Ezra. We all need a tight rein, with overcheck and crupper, too, but it doesn't help matters to abuse each other unnecessarily. There's more than one regular army officer who proved tyrannical in the extreme during the war of the Rebellion, towards raw recruits, who is sleeping on the battlefields with a mini-ball through his back. Then it seemed that it was the delight of the Westpointer to inflict punishment on the "raw recruits." Then the jailbirds were admitted to the regular army, now, you have to have a good, clean record or you can't even become a private in the army, and officers don t get shot in the back for being overbearing and tyrannical, but men from the ranks can become officers by merit.

The man who will unduly humiliate his fellowman just because he can, is on a par with Harry Thaw flogging boys for pastime.

There's Masons with whom I associate, who hated me once, and unduly wounded me because they didn't know me. They are among my best friends now, because we've gotten acquainted, and the sweetest thought of mine is, that instead of preventing their exaltation, I presented their petitions, and helped make them better men. Oh, that this spirit might settle down upon the whole world, and that instead of trying to throw stumbling-blocks in the pathway of those who are teaching God's word, and who are true disciples of the Master, that we might one and all reach out a hand and lift their loads, and offer them encouragement instead of black-cubes when they knock at our doors and ask for a tallow candle to guide them to the pathway of Christian Masonry!

A Sermon Given at the Scottish Rite

By Bascom B. Clarke

Therefore, if thou rememberest that thou hath aught against thy brother, for the love that thou bearest for Masonry, just try the remedy prescribed by the Nazarene, and great will be thy reward we are all human beings, one about as good as the rest, taking them on the average.

One day some years ago, the Commander-in-chief of Scottish Rite Masonry in Wisconsin invited me to preach a sermon to the class at the banquet following the exemplification of the work from the Fourth degree to that of Sublime Prince of the Royal Secret 32nd.

Here is what the editor of *Masonic Tidings* has to say of the event:

"The next speaker was Sublime Prince Bascom B. Clarke of Madison. The Commander-in-chief, in introducing Sublime Prince Clarke, said, 'I now introduce to you Uncle Silas who writes "The Gospel of Freemasonry" for the Masonic Tidings. He is also known as a "Funny Man," a Philosopher, and a Bishop.

"Our good brother was not disappointing in any of those roles. He created jollity and mirth by his conventional knowledge of such American phrases as a jack-pot and 'sitting in the game.' But when he turned to consider the serious things of life and cited many sad incidents in the life of the unfortunate, into whose lives had been brought hope and sunshine because of his own big heart and the Masonic brethren of Madison, and as he vividly delineated the suffering of some outcast of society, some child that had been deprived of the tender care of mother and father, and left to struggle amidst biting hunger and poverty, he awakened the deepest sympathy and touched the heart tendrils of every Sublime Prince.

"The Bishop seems to the manner-born, the very semblance of the cloth, but, dear reader, though he never was ordained a Bishop, he preaches the gospel of Humanity and God in a way that touches the hearts of mankind.

"Brother Clarke, however, is only a layman, a prominent and successful business man, who has given away a fortune — always in an unostentatious way — helping to ameliorate the sufferings of humanity. The one thought uppermost in his mind during a busy and active life — to bring sunshine into the lives of the unfortunate and those less fortunate than himself.

"We excerpt the following from his address:

" 'After four days of feasting upon the spiritual bread of life, emanating from the Sanctuary of God's Holy Temple; after the beautiful and impressive lessons which must have been deeply indented upon the trestle-board of every heart; after having been lifted higher and higher into the rose-colored ether of the spirit world, listening to the teachings of the great Sages and holy men of the past, of Confucius, Moses, Zoroaster, Mohamed, and of the Lowly Nazarene; after having assumed the most sacred vows ever taken by mortal man; after having witnessed that marvelous panorama of pictures painted upon the canvas of our immortal souls and hearing the words of truth and soberness, I wonder if we are ready at this time to turn from those holy things, to delve in thoughts of mirth and jollity; or if it were better to allow these sacred lessons and all they mean to sink deeper into our heart of hearts.

" 'The Illustrious Commander-in-chief has called me a philosopher, but my name is not Philetus. I am called "Bishop" by some who love me for what I am. I have never been consecrated a bishop excepting in the hearts of those whose hands I help to hold up in doing God's work. Last and perhaps least, I am called "The funny man of The American Thresherman" because I write stale jokes and preach sermons.

" 'One of the most serious problems in all the world is trying to be a "funny man." Why, I've paid a dollar for a seat in the bald-headed row to listen to a professional funny man, trying to make his audience smile. But my promise tonight is to tell you some serious jokes that it has been my lot to know.

" 'I began my career as a "Funny Man" publishing a very "weakly" little newspaper in an Indiana village forty years ago. It was one-half "boiler iron" insides, the other half was dedicated and devoted to dog-fights, town gossip and to teaching the correct philosophy of opening a jack-pot! In exchange for these interesting facts, I received cordwood, composed of hickory limbs that would put out a decent fire, and pumpkins from the size of a foot-ball to a wash-tub! My readers thought it was the funniest thing in the world to watch me dodging enraged neighbors and bad debt collectors. They used to gather every publication morning to read the news, and laugh when I got kicked up the stairs and down again. It's a serious business trying to be a funny man!

" 'One morning, when I had reached the limit of my credit, I turned the column rules, and between these streaks of mourning, I wrote my obituary. Then I moved. All I had to do to move was to just put out the fire and call the dog! My readers thought it was the funniest editorial I had ever written. It takes a real funny man to feel hilarious at his own funeral!

" 'Now, I 'm going to tell you why they call me "Bishop." There's a godly little man in Madison, whose wife has the face of a saint. They came there so poor in purse that they had to fertilize the barracks before they could raise a religious disturbance. My people are all Methodists, and believe in a religion that hollers. They have chased me all over their meeting houses ever since I was big enough to repeat the Lord's Prayer, trying to snare me in. They have hooked me several times, but, like our profane brethren of the class, I always back-slid.

" 'When these Volunteers of America came to do God's will, and asked me to "decorate the mahogany," their creed was so simple that I could understand. Then I invited others to "sit in," and in the polite parlance of the game I asked them to please observe the usual formalities, which means to "sugar the green" and to "sweeten the kitty."

" 'I've watched this saintly little mother at midnight's lowly hour, visiting the saloons of Madison, seining the pond for pennies and nickels with which to carry on their good work and every saloon-keeper. and every other man who says "prosit" is her friend and protector. I've watched her going alone up the dark alleys, ministering to those in need, with none to molest her.

" 'One day these Christian people told me that if they had a thousand dollars they could buy a little chapel in my ward, in which to hold religious services for the poor, and I told them to buy. They looked at me with open mouthed astonishment, and I challenged them to the "test" of God's promise to help those who keep His commands. We gave an entertainment and when the curtain raised to the strains of a calliope. everybody sang, "Nearer, My God to Thee," for we had the money in the box office with which to pay for the little chapel.

" 'One cold winter's night this godly little woman whispered to me that she had in her home a little girl, scarcely in her teens, who would soon become a mother. That she had taken from her a bottle of deadly poison with which she had meant to take her own life, because an infamous scoundrel, who should writhe in the torments of the orthodox hell, had betrayed her and left her to her fate. This good Christian woman asked me to make it possible for her to not only save this little girl's life, but her reputation as well. As "bishop" of her church, I wrote a letter, sending multigraph copies to the faithful in Madison, to some within the sound of my voice. Most of these brethren are members of this craft. I told them in an orthodox way, without disclosing my hand, that they were expected to "straddle the blind" and to tilt the lid of the official jack-pot. They filled my hands with bright, shining, smiling, glistening simoleons that talk without making a noise, and that little girl is living an upright and Christian life today, and the world knows not the secret of her life.

" 'On a hot day in July last, these same Christian people fed and watered twenty-six hundred little children in Tenney Park. The greater part of the funds for this occasion was contributed by Madison Masons. We have a wonderful photograph of that assembly of little folks, the best I have ever seen. There were white children, Norwegians, Italians, and chocolate drops. All kinds, sizes and previous conditions before being groomed for the occasion. It took a water tank to haul lemonade and a wagon to transport the sandwiches and other good things. As I looked over this crowd of Polacks, Danes, Chinese and Alligator Bait, I asked this good little woman who was managing the menagerie if she thought that all of these were included in those beautiful words, "Suffer little children and forbid them not. to come unto me, for of such is the kingdom of Heaven?" Yes, she said, they were all included in the manifest, but we'd have to scrub some of them before loading on the Old Ship of Zion.

" 'One Christmas Eve not many years ago, this whitehaired little captain rushed into my office, and after saluting me as his superior officer and as Bishop of the church, told me that he had found a home where six people were sleeping in a single bed. I asked if they were Mormons, and he said, "Come and see." I loaded a reporter for a daily paper into my automobile and with this little captain we headed for the pines. Reporters and newspaper men all enjoy funny sights. We found four little children shivering over a little stove in a home so poor that a killdeer would have had to carry his own rations. A little brown-eyed girl eleven years old, holding her baby sister, and trying to keep the others from freezing, was asked if she was looking for Santa Claus. "No," she said, "I think he is dead." That saintly Little Mother of the Volunteers of America with her own home to care for, and all the rest of "God's patient poor" in the city besides, was rushed on the job. Such a scattering of dirt and rags and such a scrubbing as that old floor received! It was such a funny sight! Why, the reporter was so amused that the tears ran down his cheeks, as we returned from the Club with a great big turkey all baked and brown, and piping hot, with cranberry sauce and oyster dressing enough to feed twenty men, as he watched those children and their parents clean the platter. It was a funny sight! It takes serious things to make some folks feel funny. We paid a return engagement of the menu for their Christmas dinner. That godly little woman made my automobile look like a moving van, loaded with bedding, clothes and clothing. At midnight when all was cleaned and when the children were asleep in clean, warm beds, we left a Christmas tree loaded with presents. It was such a good opportunity for playing a joke on those little children.

" 'Because of these little pleasantries along life's highway, they call me "Bishop." It takes funny men to make bishops. Why, Bishop Quayle of the Methodist church, who is big enough to be called a partridge, is such a funny man that he would make you laugh in administering the sacrament. But he's a tower of strength to his church and for God. I have listened to him preach and wondered how on earth he knew so much about cards, when the very disciples of the church bars him from "sitting in." I was brought up in that faith, and used to hearing, Amen, every time the preacher caught his breath. I'm still a brother-in-law and contributing member.

" 'As I listened to the answers of the brethren of the class in reply to that momentous question, over which some of us have dodged and other lied, while still others told the truth and shamed the devil, in every class, my own included, I was deeply impressed with the mirth provoking proposition, "Are you in the habit of taking God's name in vain?" It carried me back to sixteen years ago when Brother Perry and Brother Brown sat on the side lines to hear my reply. It was such a funny question that it brought a sob of shame that I had ever profaned God's Holy Name. I wasn't like George Washington who couldn't tell a lie. I dared not, for I knew that I'd get caught in it. The hand pressure from those brethren who were watching me there, for having told the truth, was comforting indeed. "Who doesn't know whether or not he takes God's name in vain?" No man on this earth, with his reason not dethroned, but who knows only too well whether he takes God's name in vain or not. Every man who does not swear is justly proud of the fact, and those who do swear feel the cutting humility as you and I, my profane brethren, have felt when that question has been plainly put to us. To lie about it is compounding a felony, even though such a question could cause a smile or sneer from any man! It takes serious things to make some men feel funny, now, doesn't it?

" 'As I watched the temptation of Zerubbabel, writhing under the tempter's plea, and heard his prayer before the Ark of the Covenant, where the Shekinah had come down from Heaven and lighted up the Ark between the wings of the Cherubim, for strength to withstand the great temptation, as I saw him triumph because of his fidelity, in my soul I said, "Blessed be the God of Truth!"

" 'As a philosopher I commend to you the example of Philetus, as a serious man I warn you of the hazard of trying to win the pot in poker on a single pair, as a Bishop who has never been consecrated, I raise my hands and invoke the blessing of the Holy Trinity to rest and abide with you each and every one.'"

If all men were perfect there would be no need of church or Masonic revivals, there would be no need of courts or jails, no need of great armies clashing in a world's war, but all men and women could dwell together in unity, meeting on the level, acting by the plumb-line, and parting, on the square.

www.ingramcontent.com/pod-product-compliance
Lightning Source LLC
LaVergne TN
LVHW041459070426
835507LV00009B/701